TWO-FOOT GAUGE SURVIVORS

A tour of historic 60cm passenger railways of the English speaking world

Vic Mitchell

Cover pictures: *Steam traction extremes: 0-4-0ST Prince was built in 1863 for the pioneering Festiniog Railway and still works on the line. Weighing only eight tons when constructed, it can be compared with the 61-ton 2-6-2 + 2-6-2 Garratt, which came from Hanomag in 1928 and was no. 81 on South African Railway's Avontuur branch. (F.Boughey and D.J.Mitchell)*

Published August 1998

ISBN 1 901706 21 4

© *Middleton Press, 1998*

Design Deborah Goodridge

Published by
    Middleton Press
    Easebourne Lane
    Midhurst, West Sussex
    GU29 9AZ
Tel: 01730 813169
Fax: 01730 812601

Printed & bound by Biddles Ltd,
    Guildford and Kings Lynn

CONTENTS

India
1. Darjeeling Himalayan Railway
2. Matheran Railway
3. Scindia State Railway

South Africa
4. Avontuur Branch
5. Alfred County Railway

Wales
6. Vale of Rheidol Railway
7. Festiniog Railway

INDEX

Aberffrwd	6.6	Loerie	4.20
Aberystwyth	6.1	Mahanadi	1.11
Assegaaibos	4.30	Minffordd	7.16
Avontuur	4.32	Neral	2.1
Blaenau Ffestiniog	7.27	New Jalpaiguri	1.1
Boston Lodge Works	7.10	Nonera	3.5
Capel Bangor	6.5	Paddock	5.15
Chelsea	4.15	Patensie	4.26
Darjeeling	1.22	Plains	5.14
Dduallt	7.22	Port Elizabeth -	
Devils Bridge	6.7	Cement Works	4.10
Gamtoos	4.23	Harbour	4.1
Ghum	1.18	Humewood Rd	4.4
Gwalior	3.1	Port Shepstone	5.1
Hankey	4.27	Portmadoc Harbour	7.1
Harding	5.18	Siliguri Junction	1.2
Humansdorp	4.28	Tan-y-Bwlch	7.20
Izotsha	5.13	Tanygrisiau	7.25
Joubertina	4.31	Tindharia	1.4
Jumma Patti	2.6	Two Streams	4.29
Kurseong	1.12	Van Stadens	4.17
Llyn Ystradau	7.26	Waterpipe	2.7

ACKNOWLEDGEMENTS

In addition to those mentioned in the photographic credits, I have received much help from the following and for that I am very grateful: P.Burton, J.Crosby, B.Cawkwell, K.Dakin, N.Gurley, M.Hudson, G.Ive, Mrs B.Mitchell, R.Mitchell, B.Minnaar, C.Muller, Mr D. & Dr S.Salter, I.Simpson, Dr G.Sutton, M.Swift and N.Thompson.

INTRODUCTION

EVOLUTION OF TWO-FOOT GAUGE

The term two-foot gauge in this volume is used to include railways from 22 to 24 ins (56 to 61 cms).

North Wales had slate quarry railways of about 2 ft gauge from the early part of the nineteenth century; from Penrhyn in 1801 and from Dinorwic in 1825. No explanation for the use of this dimenson is known.

The desire to link a group of slate quarries further south to a new harbour on the Cambrian coast resulted in an Act of Parliament in 1832 for the construction of the Festiniog Railway, to a gauge of "under three feet". Downhill traffic was worked by gravity and horses were used uphill but, in the early years, there were two inclines on the route as well.

The FR made news in the railway engineering world in 1863 when it successfully applied steam traction to this small gauge, contrary to the earlier opinions of notable engineers such as Robert Stephenson. A further unique and major development took place on this remote and isolated little railway in 1865 when passenger conveyance commenced. Consent for this involved approval by one of Her Majesty's Board of Trade inspecting officers of railways, Captain H.W.Tyler RE. He considered this such a remarkable and unusual development that he took the rare step of addressing the Institution of Civil Engineers on the subject.

Since the Gauge Act in 1846, Britsh legislation had demanded that most new passenger lines be of standard 4ft 8½ins gauge. Despite Tyler's great enthusiasm for narrow gauge, British politicians did not see fit to encourage its development within home shores. However, his words fell on fertile soil overseas.

Another narrow gauge protagonist at that time was the inventive engineer, Robert Fairlie, whose patent for a double engine was so dramatically demonstrated on the Festiniog Railway in 1869-72. *Little Wonder* had central controls and two fireboxes, situated mid-way in a long boiler which was supported on two powered bogies. It showed that very heavy trains could be hauled over cheaply constructed contour-hugging narrow gauge lines.

Demonstrations were given on the FR, encouraged by the enterprising Charles Spooner, then its engineer and manager. Delegations arrived in this distant corner of the Principality from around the world, notably from France, Germany, Imperial Russia, India, Hungary, Norway and Sweden.

As is so common in our engineering history, British inventiveness and originality had to be developed abroad owing to the stifling actions of politicians. Then, as now, they thought they knew best about the future of the country's railways and refused to listen to the specialists. It was to be 1896 before they belatedly reconsidered the matter of gauge and passed the Light Railways Act, another case of parliamentarians "shutting the stable door after the horse had bolted". The Act was intended to encourage the construction of low-cost railways in districts that had suffered economic hardships as a result of poor transport and any gauge could be considered.

By about 1910, the general traffic narrow gauge railway had spread world-wide from its birthplace in Wales, two-foot lines eventually being particularly successful in parts of India and Southern Africa, where British influence was dominant.

Following the French practice, the dimension of one foot eleven and five eighths inches (60cms) was adopted as the standard for the British Army narrow gauge network in World War I. Surplus military track sold after hostilities ceased resulted in this gauge becoming common for industrial and agricultural railways, in both countries.

SOME NOTABLE BYGONES

Difficult terrain was the usual reason for choosing minimal gauge, but such areas normally meant low population density and hence poor passenger potential. However, such terrain has proved the salvation of most of the survivors described herein, as the scenery has generated tourist traffic. Little attempt has been made to show this aspect of the railways herein.

A notable British two-foot gauge route to be built soon after the 1896 Act (but with its own Act) was the Lynton & Barnstaple Railway in Devon. Sadly this succumbed to competition from road transport in 1935, having become part of the Southern Railway in 1923.

Less notable was the seven mile long Ashover Railway in Derbyshire, which opened in 1925 but ceased to carry passengers in 1936, although it survived until 1950.

A rare exception to the rule regarding new non-standard lines was the North Wales Narrow Gauge Railways which opened seven miles of its main route in 1877 and a further five to South Snowdon (Rhyd Ddu) in 1881. After a chequered history, which included extension south to Portmadoc (21 route miles, 33km) under the title of Welsh Highland Railway, it closed to passengers in 1936 and to goods in the following year. The present WHR lines cannot be considered to be survivors.

Our nearest continental 60cm system is worthy of note as two of its steam trains were stopped literally in their tracks by bombs during the unexpected invasion of Normandy on 6th June 1944. The Chemin de fer de Calvados was begun in 1891 and at its optimum comprised 135 route miles (217km). The lines in the vicinity of Bayeux closed in 1928-35 but some in the Caen area were still in use during the German occupation, having reverted to steam operation due to fuel shortage for the petrol electric Crochat railcars.

There was little interest in the two-foot gauge in the USA. However, one line, almost ten miles in length, was opened in Massachusetts in September 1877. The engineer of the Billerica & Bedford Railroad, George E. Mansfield, had (sensibly) spent part of his UK honeymoon visiting the Festiniog Railway, but his brainchild failed commercially and was closed in June 1878. Undeterred, he purchased the rolling stock and became involved in establishing the Sandy River Railroad in Maine in 1879. This became part of a system of lumber railways which totalled 101 miles (161km) in length by 1908. The FR influence could be seen here until closure in 1935. Also in Maine was the 54-mile (86km) long Wiscasset, Waterville & Farmington Railroad which was in use from 1895 until 1937. This was a Mansfield inspired line, as was the Bridgton & Saco River Railroad, a 21-mile (33km) route which struggled on until 1941.

The Beira Railway was one of the most ambitious two-foot gauge railways in Africa, indeed the whole world. At its fullest extent it connected the port of Beira, on the Indian Ocean, with Umtali, Rhodesia, and provided the British colony with a vital lifeline to the sea. The choice of two-foot gauge for a railway 222 miles (355km) long is remarkable and the clouded history of the line earns it the sobriquet of "The two foot gauge enigma". (This is also the title of a recent book on the line from Plateway Press).

The railway was conceived in 1890 - at a time when Rhodesia had no rail communication at all - and required intense diplomatic pressure on Portugal (the Colonial power controlling Mozambique) to allow a railway across its territory. Construction began in 1892. Driven through unexplored bush and unhealthy swamps in the short space of six years, the railway extracted a terrible toll in human life. Sixty percent of the white staff perished from fever - construction of one bridge alone cost the lives of seven engineers - and it was said that one Indian or Chinese labourer died for every sleeper laid. As well as a hostile climate, and clouds of disease-bearing mosquitoes, the contractors had to cope with the depredations of lions, elephants and crocodiles. Despite this, the line reached the Rhodesian border in October 1897 and full opening to Umtali took place in February 1898.

The Beira Railway's finest hour came during the Boer War when it was used to rush 5000 Australian and New Zealand troops, their 1000 horses and assorted stores to the defence of Rhodesia. However, the rapid development of Southern Africa soon overwhelmed the capacity of the two-foot gauge, and in 1900 the line was relaid to 3ft 6ins. This became standard gauge for the area, although only six inches wider than 95% of USA "narrow gauge" lines. (Three feet was Fairlie's preferred dimension).

A once-extensive system in Namibia (South West Africa) vanished in 1959-60, but much of the rolling stock was transferred to other lines in South Africa. Of those in Natal, on the east coast, three out of four closed completely in 1983-86, again resulting in transfer of stock.

Yugoslavia had an extensive 600mm system until 1966. A journey on the 75mile (120km) main line used to consume 10 hours. Poland still has a number of lines of this gauge in regular use.

The Lynton & Barnstaple 2-6-2T *Lew* was recorded entering the terminus at Lynton with the 3.15pm from Barnstaple on 6th September 1933. (K.Nunn/LCGB)

REVIVALS, NEW LINES AND OTHER SURVIVORS

Slowly returning to life after about two decades of closure is a remarkable line on the east coast of Greece. It ran east from Volos, the fourth largest city in that country, through the streets and then along the beautiful coast of the Gulf of Pagasae for seven and three quarter miles (12.4km) to Ano Lechonia. This tramway was opened in 1896 and was extended in 1903 as a railway for 10 miles (16km) to Mileai. This involved climbing almost continuously at 1 in 33 to reach this small town which is situated 750 ft (228m) above sea level.

There was little freight traffic, wagons sometimes being attached to passenger trains. Total closure took place on 20th June 1971, but most of the equipment remained in place. There were reports of some activity on parts of the coastal line in the early 1990s and of some regular trains by 1994. In the Summer of 1996, there was one trip each way on the hilly western section on Saturdays, Sundays and public holidays only. Although there is a lack of publicity and information, there are plans to reopen to Volos, although probably not the tarred-over street section.

In Poland, the once extensive Kleinbahn Znin, which had four lines radiating from Znin, survives in part. The network was created in stages between 1893 and 1950, and served scattered agricultural communities. Passenger services were withdrawn in 1963 but sugar beet continued to be carried into the 1990s.

Following the fall of the Iron Curtain in 1990, tourism grew and this justified the introduction of a steam-hauled service in the Summer over the original section of the route. It operated for nearly 4 miles (6km) in 1997, both north and south of Wenecja, where a narrow gauge museum containing fourteen 600mm gauge locomotives had been established. There were three trips northwards and six southwards. Although the landscape is fairly flat, there are a number of attractive lakes in the area.

Elsewhere a number of redundant indus-trial and agricultural two-foot gauge lines have been adapted for tourism. Some new lines have been laid on former standard gauge trackbeds, notable in Britain being the Bala Lake Railway, the Brecon Mountain Railway, the Launceston Steam Railway, the South Tynedale Railway, the Welsh Highland Railway (Porthmadog) and the Welsh Highland Railway (Caernarfon). Of the last two, the former is on the bed of a siding, three quarters of a mile (1.2km) long, and the latter is on a 3 mile (5km) route last used in 1964. The two envisage the rebuilding of the intervening section of the original WHR, which closed in receivership in 1936. The distance is about 23 miles (37km).

Submitted to a Public Inquiry at Chichester in West Sussex in April 1998 (by your author) was a proposal for up to four miles (6.4km) of two-foot gauge lines for the conveyance of unprocessed gravel in an area where road transport is problematical. A potential use of part of the system by passengers has been identified. As the anti-lorry lobby grows, so does the likelihood of a revival of local two-foot gauge mineral railways, but in a modern and energy efficient form. Maybe the "Mitchell Mineral Mover" (Treble M) will become a reality and be applied more widely, illustrating again that the two-foot gauge is not only ideal for the carriage of divisible loads, but is the maximum gauge required and thus the most economic.

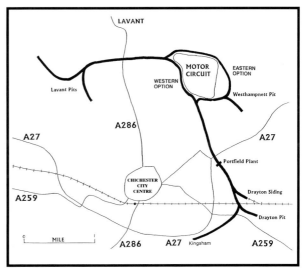

1. DARJEELING HIMALAYAN RAILWAY
Lawrence Marshall

Until 1814 Darjeeling, then part of Sikkim, was virtually unknown. In that year the British owned East India Company, appreciating the cool climate of the Himalayan foothills, commenced the development of the village. In 1835 the by then much enlarged town was selected as a sanatorium for British troops serving in India but the cart road from the plains at Siliguri up to Darjeeling was hopelessly inadequate. By this time tea was being grown in the area and processed on a large scale but the difficulties of transport remained.

In 1878 the Assam Bengal Railway reached Siliguri from Calcutta and a steam tramway up to Darjeeling was planned. Work commenced a year later and despite fearsome geographical difficulties Kurseong had been reached by August 1880 and Darjeeling by July 1881, a total distance of 51 miles. The British owned Darjeeling Himalayan Railway Company Limited was purchased by the Indian Government in 1948.

The railway basically follows the route of the old cart road and has a ruling gradient of 1 in 25 but occasionally as steep as 1 in 20. To gain height at difficult locations there are three loops and five zig zags. The line was extended eastwards in 1964 from Siliguri to New Jalpaiguri to connect with the new broad gauge line to Assam. Between Siliguri and Darjeeling there are only three stations of any importance, Tindharia at 2822 feet and the adminstrative headquarters of the line, Kurseong at 4864 feet and Ghum at 7407 feet, the highest point on the line. Darjeeling is situated at 6812 feet above sea level. With a maximum speed limit of 12mph the present one advertised through train per day takes eight and a half hours, mishaps permitting. There is also the "school train" which does an out and back journey each day from Kurseong to Darjeeling. Due to the fragile state of the locomotives present day loads are limited to three coaches. Sadly passenger traffic is at a low level and freight traffic is virtually non existent, a review of the future of the line is due in the year 2000 and the outlook is bleak. However, the Railway Board in New Delhi now appreciate the historical importance of this amazing railway and local residents, particularly the tea estate owners and hoteliers, realise how important the line is as a tourist attraction.

Motive power on the Darjeeling Railway has always been provided by 0-4-0 tank locomotives, mostly of the saddle tank variety. However, Beyer Peacock & Co supplied a Garratt type engine in 1910 but it was not a success. Two neat "Pacific" type tender locomotives came from the North British Locomotive Company in 1914 but these were built specifically for the 66 mile Kishanganj extension railway, which opened in 1915 and was converted to metre gauge in 1949. There was also a 29 mile branch from Siliguri to Kalimpong Road (for Kalimpong) known as the Teesta Valley railway, this opened in 1914 and closed in 1950 following severe flooding of the Teesta river. The surviving line traverses flat country at the outset and then enters an area of forests and tea estates. After Tindharia, where the locomotive and carriage works and main locomotive shed are situated, there are less trees to be seen but fine views of the Himalayan foothills open up as the line twists and turns to Kurseong. Here there is a long stop to allow refreshments for the passengers and the servicing of the valiant little blue B class saddle tank, which will have taken the train over at Tindharia. After reversing the train out of Kurseong station the train then threads its way through the bazaar area of the town before heading into open country. Shortly after leaving Ghum, superb views of the Eastern Himalayas can be seen from the famous double loop at Batasia; on a clear day twelve peaks, all over 20,000 feet high, are visible. The tallest is Kanchenjunga towering to 28,146 feet, the third highest mountain in the world.

This is a unique railway, go there if you can, you will not regret it. The line now forms part of the Northeast Frontier Railway of Indian Railways.

An order for some new steam locomotives was announced in 1998.

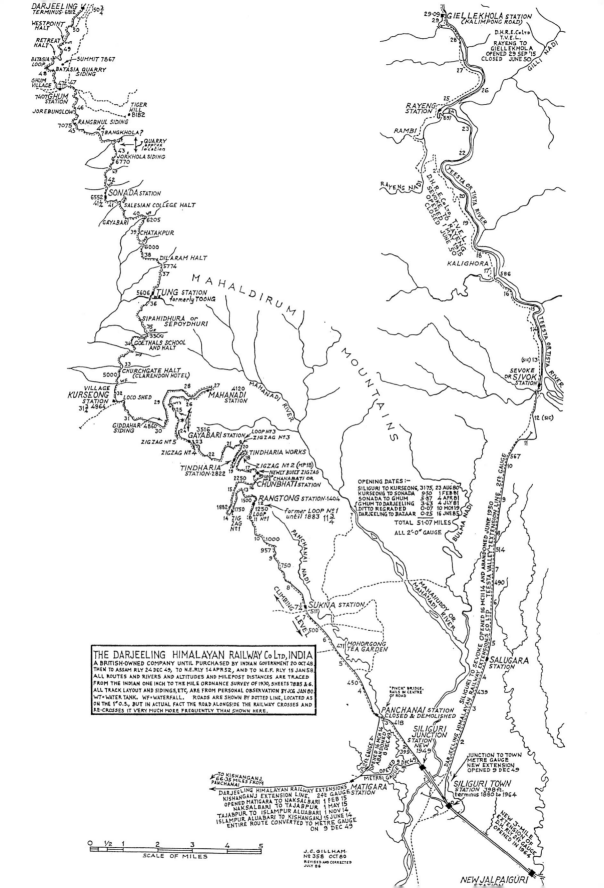

NEW JALPAIGURI

1.1 New Jalpaiguri depot was photographed on the 18th November 1974, and seen on the left is C class Pacific no. 808 built for the Kishanganj extension railway; on the right is B class no. 797, one of three of this famous design built at Tindharia workshops in 1925. (L.G.Marshall).

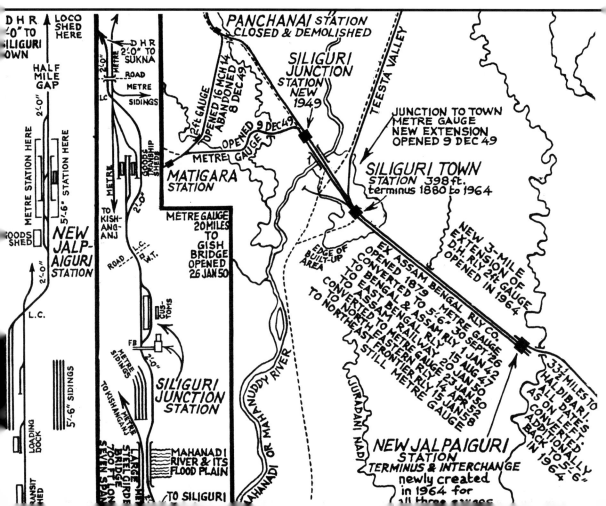

1.2 Late arriving passenger! As the 7.00 departure for Darjeeling pulls out of New Jalpaiguri about an hour late on the 3rd March 1993, a last minute passenger thumbs the train down. The engine is B class no 795. New Jalpaiguri is unusual in having three gauges, five foot six inch, metre and two foot. Metre gauge coaches can be seen in the background. (L.G.Marshall).

SILIGURI JUNCTION

1.3 No. 790 was recorded at Siliguri Junction on the 11th November 1970 after arrival on the first train of the morning from Darjeeling to New Jalpaiguri. The low roof line of the third coach looks decidedly odd, but the locomotive is spotless. (L.G.Marshall).

TINDHARIA

1.4 In 1984 Laurie Marshall ran the fifth of his eight GREAT INDIAN TRAIN JOURNEYS and a special was arranged, free of charge, from New Jalpaiguri to Darjeeling. B class no. 800 took the first stage to Tindharia; here she awaits departure from Rangtong on the morning of the 29th February. Observe the very small covered station area. (L.G.Marshall)

1.5 On the FIRST GREAT INDIAN TRAIN JOURNEY B class no 779, suitably adorned, was the motive power from New Jalpaiguri to Tindharia, here the train is seen entering the loop at the south end of Tindharia station on the 24th November 1978. (L.G.Marshall).

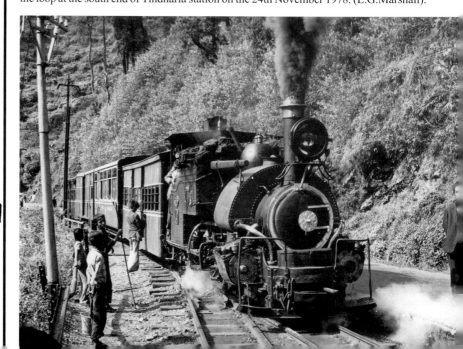

1.6 The main entrance to the Darjeeling Railway workshops is seen on the morning of 20th November 1974, and the original B class engine, no 777, is being pulled out by sister no 790 ready for filming by the BBC 2 team making the film ROMANCE OF INDIAN RAILWAYS. It was shown in 1975 in the WORLD ABOUT US series. No 777 now resides in the National Railway Museum in New Delhi. (L.G.Marshall).

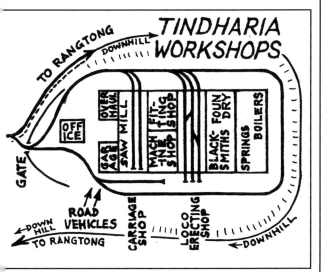

NEW JALPAIGURI—DARJEELING						
UP			(Narrow Gauge).		DOWN	
3 D Pass. 1. 2.	1 D Pass. 1. 2.	9 D Pass. 2nd.	STATIONS.	4 D Pass. 1. 2.	2 D Pass. 1. 2.	10 D Pass. 2nd.
H. M.	H. M.	H. M.		H. M.	H. M.	H. M.
7 15	9 0		d New Jalpaiguri a	16 20	17 45	—
7 30	9 15		,, Siliguri Town ,,	15 50	17 25	
7 45	9 30		a Siliguri Jn. {d	15 40	17 15	
7 50	9 35		d a	15 35	16 55	
8 1	10 2		,, Sukna ,,	15 3	16 23	
9 1	10 46		,, Rangtong ,,	14 23	15 43	
9 43	11 20		,, Chunbhati ,,	13 48	15 5	
10 10	11 55		,, Tindharia ,,	13 11	14 39	
10 49	12 34		,, Gayabari ,,	12 25	14 0	
11 25	13 9		,, Mahanadi ,,	11 49	13 24	
12 32	14 6	...	a Kurseong {d	11 10	12 47	
12 42	14 16	6 40	d a	11 5	12 37	19 0
...	...	6 49	,, Churchgate Halt	...	...	18 45
...	...	7 2	,, Goethals Halt ,,	...	...	18 32
...	...	7 14	,, Sopoydhuri ... ,,	...	...	18 20
13 20	14 54	7 24	,, Tung. a.. ,,	10 26	11 58	18 10
...	...	7 40	,, Dilaram Halt ,,	...	...	17 58
...	...	7 59	,, Salesian College	...	...	17 50
14 3	15 37	8 11	,, Sonada ,,	9 47	11 15	17 30
...	...	...	,, Jorekhola Siding	...	...	17 23
...	...	8 45	,, Rangbhul Siding	...	...	16 54
...	...	8 50	,, Jorebunglow ,,	...	...	16 49
14 50	16 25	9 5	,, Ghum ... ,,	9 0	10 33	16 20
...	...	...	,, Batasia Siding	...	...	...
...	...	...	,, Retreat Halt ,,	...	...	...
...	...	9 30	,, WestpointHalt ,,	...	...	15 55
15 30	17 30	9 45	a Darjeeling... d	8 25	10 0	15 45

NORTH OF TINDHARIA

1.7 There are five zig zags on the Darjeeling railway, this is No 3 just above Tindharia station and no. 797 is negotiating the first part. Passing the green flag the train will enter a headshunt, the points will be changed and the train will make a spirited charge up the slope to gain the road at the top on 25th November 1978. (L.G.Marshall).

1.8 An easier way to gain altitude was to build a loop. This is loop No 3, also known as "agony point", which lies between Tindharia and Gayabari stations. The three coach train is heading for Darjeeling and was photographed in February 1987. (N.F.Gurley).

1.9 Shortly after Gayabari, water is taken from the hillside at Pagla Jhora. In dappled light no. 799 on a longer than usual train from New Jalpaiguri to Darjeeling takes her fill on the 11th of November 1970. The passengers are enjoying the tranquility and the sweeping views across the foothills. Monkeys are a particular problem at this stopping point. (L.G.Marshall).

1.10 No. 792 climbs steeply out of Pagla Jhora on the morning train from New Jalpaiguri to Darjeeling on 20th November 1974. In the monsoon season water cascades down the rock face in the background causing considerable problems. Apart from the driver and fireman, there are two men to apply sand under the wheels of the engine and a man sitting on the coal to break it and pass it back through the cab windows! (L.G.Marshall).

MAHANADI

1.11 Full speed through the streets! The daily train from New Jalpaiguri to Darjeeling charges through the main bazaar area of the little town of Mahanadi hauled by B class no 782 on 2nd March 1993. (L.G.Marshall).

KURSEONG

1.12 The small locomotive shed at Kurseong is seen on 17th November 1983 with "the grand old lady", B class no 779 awaiting her next turn of duty. Built in 1892 she was, at that time, the oldest working engine on Indian Railways, and still is. (L.G.Marshall).

1.13 In the 1970s freight workings were quite common; here is no. 801 at Kurseong sidings after arrival from Tindharia on 6th November, 1970. (L.G.Marshall).

1.14 By the 1980s freight traffic on the Darjeeling Railway was minimal. This picture was taken on 9th January 1980 and shows the goods sidings at Kurseong looking downhill towards Tindharia. The little locomotive depot, normally home to one locomotive overnight, can be see in the left background. Observe the road competition on the right. (J.C.Gillham).

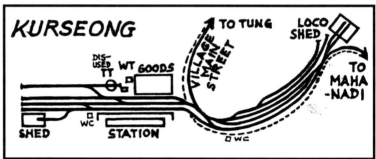

1.15 On reaching Kurseong the train veers off into the tiny terminal station, where passengers and locomotive take on liquids. The fire is raked out and then no. 788 sets back into the main street before heading through the bazaar area en route to Darjeeling. The date is 5th November 1970. (L.G.Marshall).

1.16 A general view of Kurseong shows the station on the afternoon of 8th January 1980. No. 788 has arrived on the morning train from the plains to Darjeeling; the disused turntable can be seen on the left and the very hilly nature of Kurseong is evident from the houses in the background. The same engine shown in the previous picture is seen almost exactly ten years later. (J.C.Gillham).

1.17 Kurseong and no. 788 yet again. Here she is heading along the side of the former "cart road" between Siliguri and Darjeeling with a van train, the local population are quite used to this sight but it does not enhance the whiteness of their laundry visible in the background on 6th November 1970 (L.G.Marshall).

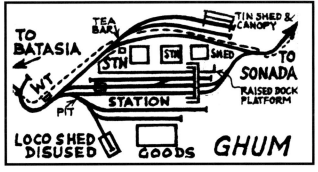

GHUM

1.18 The highest point on the Darjeeling Railway is at Ghum, 7407 feet above sea level. This view is looking downhill towards Kurseong on 9th January 1980; there is an island platform with a tiny refreshment room and several sidings. A train heading downhill can be seen on the right hand side of the platform. (J.C.Gillham).

SOUTH OF DARJEELING

1.19 Apart from the once daily through train from New Jalpaiguri to Darjeeling, there is the "school train" which leaves Kurseong at 6.40 in the morning and, if lucky, arrives at Darjeeling at 9.45. In this picture no. 779 is crossing the little bridge at the start of the famous double loop at Bhatasia on 17th November 1983. (L.G.Marshall).

1.20 Panoramic view of the double loop at Bhatasia in February 1987 includes the "school train" negotiating the upper circuit. The views from here are superb. If it is cloudy (it often is), there is a painting of the eastern Himalayas on the board in the bottom left hand corner of the picture. The lower loop can clearly be seen on the right of the photograph. (N.F.Gurley).

1.21 Trains from Darjeeling down to the plains always run bunker first. From Darjeeling, seen here, to Bhatasia loop the line climbs almost 600 feet, thereafter the train drifts most of the way down to Sukna. The bad weather sheeting on the rear of the cab can be very essential but it seems to belong to no. 805, rather than the engine seen, no. 798! (N.F.Gurley).

DARJEELING

1.22 A picture from the 1921 official guide to DARJEELING and its MOUNTAIN RAILWAY shows the terminus in about 1920. The locomotive and carriage shed can be discerned on the left. The present station at Darjeeling has a similar track layout but there is no overall canopy to the platforms and the main building now has a flat roof. Sadly it is no longer as tidy and there has been much commercial development in the vicinity.

1.23 Darjeeling has a large covered locomotive and carriage shed. In this picture taken on a gloomy afternoon on 10th November 1970, we see no. 779 cold in the depot and no. 793 being serviced. (L.G.Marshall).

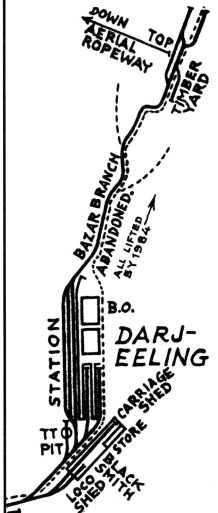

1.24 The locomotive and carriage sheds at Darjeeling are close to the station (left). Blowing off on 9th January 1980 is a B class engine. (J.C.Gillham).

1.25 Here we view Darjeeling station and look uphill towards the Bazaar area of the town on 9th January 1980. Two B class engines appear on the left hand side of the picture and the disused turntable is also evident. Although there are three platforms only the left hand one sees departures and arrivals except at very busy times. (J.C.Gillham).

1.26 A downhill panorama of Darjeeling station includes the station canopies which were built after World War II and the platform shown is the one normally used. Some of the inevitable "Indian Railway Dogs" appear on the right of the picture taken on 9th January 1980. (J.C.Gillham).

1.27 In happier times when the down train to New Jalpaiguri ran in more than one part nos 780 and 799 await departure from Darjeeling on the morning of 21st November 1974. One of several Tibetan monasteries in the area can be seen in the background, plus a small portion of the Hotel Kanchanjunga. (L.G.Marshall).

2. MATHERAN RAILWAY
Lawrence Marshall

Neral, situated 53 miles south east of Bombay (now known as Mumbai) lies on the former Great Indian Peninsula Railway route to Central and Southern India. It is the railhead, depot and workshops for the Matheran Railway which connects the searingly hot plains of India and the sticky heat of Bombay with the coolness of the hill resort of Matheran in the Western Ghats. The pronunciation is MAT-HER-AN.

The original railway was British owned and was titled the Matheran Steam Tramway Co. Ltd. It opened to traffic in 1907 and the motive power was four attractive 0-6-0 tank locomotives built by Orenstein & Koppel between 1905 and 1907. Their construction was supervised by E.R.Calthrop & Partners of Leek & Manifold Railway fame. These engines had Klein-Lindener flexible frames for negotiating the extremely sharp curves which abound on the line. In the late 1960s, five 2ft 6ins gauge diesel locomotives were transferred from the Kalka-Simla section of the Northern Railway and regauged. These formed the mainstay of the motive power, with steam used at busy times or to prior order from visiting railway enthusiasts. In addition there was a 14-seat petrol railcar, with chain and sprocket drive; it was built in 1927 and now resides in the Indian Railway Museum in New Delhi. Sadly steam traction finished in the late 1980s and the locomotives have been "plinthed" or sold.

Starting at 121 feet above sea level, the 12.6 mile line climbs to a height of 2484 feet to reach Matheran. The journey takes two hours and there are four trains per day in each direction. The timetable states there are no trains during June to September (the monsoon season) but extra trains can be run at times of peak traffic. A heavy surcharge, by Indian standards, is made due to the difficult and expensive operating conditions. It is best to visit the railway during the week; at weekends half of Bombay seems to be there.

The scenery along the line is dry and rugged with little vegetation but there are fine views of the Western Ghats. From Neral the lofty Matheran Hill can be seen and it appears impossible for a train to reach the summit. There are two intermediate statons, Jumma Patti at 801 feet and Waterpipe at 1605 feet. In steam days both were watering points. Between these two stations is a tunnel labelled at each end "One kiss tunnel" The line is well worth a visit and makes a good day out from Bombay.

NERAL

2.1 Ready for the morning run up into the Western Ghats. MLR class Orenstein & Koppel 0-6-0T's nos. 740 and 738 alongside the 14 seater petrol railcar no 898 at the three platform terminus at Neral on 21st November 1980. The railcar was fitted with chain and sprocket drive; it was built in 1927 and now resides in the Indian Railway Museum in New Delhi. (L.G.Marshall)

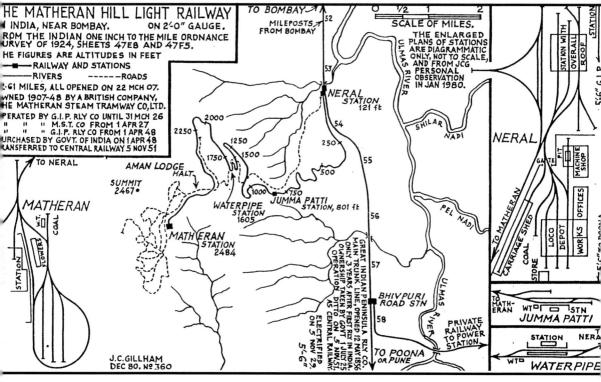

2.2 The entrance to the combined steam, diesel and petrol railcar depot at Neral is seen on 29th December 1979. The line up to Matheran is on the right. (J.C.Gillham)

2.3 A very well patronised morning train departs from Neral for the summit on 29th December 1979. Former Kalka-Simla Railway regauged diesel locomotive no 504 is in charge.(J.C.Gillham)

2.4 The three types of Matheran Railway motive power were photographed at Neral depot on 11th March 1973. NDM class diesel no. 502 is on the left, MLR class no. 741 is in the centre and is followed by the petrol railcar no. 898. The specific headboard on the diesel is interesting. Up trains come down the hill!(L.G.Marshall)

2.5 Two miniscule four wheeled vehicles plus a bogie coach were photographed at Neral on 11th March 1973. All three had just returned on a 5ft 6ins gauge wagon from the Central Railway carriage shops at Parel, Bombay. The four-wheeled van is part of the Matheran Railway breakdown train.(L.G.Marshall)

JUMMA PATTI

2.6 Just below Jumma Patti station lies the sharpest curve on the line. MLR class No 740 tried to go straight ahead with disastrous results on the morning of 21st November 1980; rerailing took about an hour.(L.G.Marshall)

WATERPIPE

2.7 The appropriately named Waterpipe station is viewed towards Matheran. An up train to Neral is on the right on 29th November 1979. (J.C.Gillham)

2.8 Another view of Waterpipe station is included but this time looking downhill towards Neral. MLR class no 738 is heading for the summit at Matheran on 29 December 1979.(J.C.Gillham)

MATHERAN

2.9 Both the hill resort of Matheran and its narrow gauge terminus are charming. No. 738 has just arrived on a morning train from Neral and the coaches are being cleaned. To turn and face right way round on the downhill journey the steam locomotives ran round a pear-shaped loop and then backed on to the train.(L.G.Marshall)

Timetable for October 1991. Note-In addition to the scheduled trains mentioned, arrangements will be made to run additional trains as and when traffic justifies.

2.10 The station at Matheran was photographed on 29th December 1979. The loop mentioned in the previous picture curved away from the far end of the platform, three sidings being accommodated within it. The locomotive is no. 738. (J.C.Gillham)

3. SCINDIA STATE RAILWAY
Lawrence Marshall

The extremely wealthy and powerful Indian princes frequently paid for the construction of narrow gauge railways to serve their people and the Maharajah Scindia of Gwalior was no exception. Starting in 1899, he developed three two-foot gauge lines radiating out of the city of Gwalior in the state now known as Madhya Pradesh. These lines ran to Bhind in the north east, west to Sheopur Kalan and south west to Shivpuri serving a large wildlife area. The line to Bhind, opened in 1899, is 52 miles in length and runs through rather uninteresting flat scenery. There are two mixed diesel trains per day in each direction and these cross at Nonera. The line to Sheopur Kalan, opened 1904-09 is much longer at 125 miles; the single journey takes ten hours by "mixed express" or eight and a half hours on the three times weekly diesel railcar, not a line to traverse "out and back" in one day! The line to Shivpuri closed quite a few years ago; it was even longer.

Early motive power consisted of small engines built mainly by Kerr Stuart & Co of Stoke-on-Trent and this supplier continued to build for the Scindia Maharajahs until 1928. In later years, before the Central Railway dieselised the two lines, the locomotive stock consisted of five 2-8-2 designs, including four engines built by Nippon Shharyo of Japan as recently as 1959, four very handsome 4-6-4s from Kerr Stuart & Co and six 4-6-2s from Bagnalls of Stafford. All seven types were tender engines and quite massive for such a small gauge. Heavy repairs for the steam stock were, in later years, carried out at Kurduwadi, the headquarters of the 2ft 6ins gauge former Barsi Light Railway.

The lines are now part of the Central Railway of Indian Railways and we visit the lower part of the shorter one.

GWALIOR

3.1 The ND class 4-6-4 tender engines were fine looking machines. Four were supplied by Kerr Stuart in 1928; no. 744 awaits departure from Gwalior on the afternoon train to Bhind on 29th November 1975, the front balcony being for the benefit of the photographer. The line to Bhind left from the west side of Gwalior station in a southerly direction and then curved through 270 degrees to pass under the Central Railway main line from Jhansi to Agra at the north end of the station. Banking assistance was frequently needed.(L.G.Marshall)

	GWALIOR—BHIND (Narrow Gauge).								
K.M.	STATIONS.		557 Diesel Mxd. 2nd.	659 Diesel Mxd. 2nd.	STATIONS.		660 Diesel Mxd. 2nd.	658 Diesel Mxd. 2nd.	
	S. p. 204, 228		H. M.	H. M.			H. M.	H. M.	
...	Gwalior Jn.	d	15 0	7 15	Bhind	d	6 25	14 30	
4	Golzka-Mandir	,,	15 17	7 *32	Itehar	,,	6 54	14 59	
13	Shadroli	,,	15 45	8 0	Asokhar	,,	7 11	15 16	
20	Sanichara	,,	16 6	8 21	Soni	,,	7 27	15 32	
26	Rethora-Kalan	,,	16 22	8 36	Sondha Road	,,	7 50	15 55	
33	Nonera	,,	16 48	9 0	Gohad Road	,,	8 12	16 17	
44	Gohad Road	,,	17 34	9 37	Nonera	,,	8 51	16 57	
52	Sondha Road	,,	17 59	10 2	Rethora Kalan	,,	9 23	17 18	
61	Soni	,,	18 21	10 24	Sanichara	,,	9 41	17 36	
66	Asokhar	,,	18 38	10 41	Shadroli	,,	10 3	17 58	
72	Itehar	,,	18 55	10 58	Golaxa-Mandir	,,	10 30	18 25	
84	Bhind	,,	19 40	11 40	Gwalior Jn.	,,	11 5	18 55	

3.2 Class NH/3 locomotives of the Scindia State Railway were almost identical to the ND class and were built in the same year, but the wheel arrangement was 2-8-2. Designed mainly for goods traffic, they regularly shared duties on passenger trains with the 4-6-2 and 4-6-4 types. No 753 is shunting the diminutive Wickham railcar, built in 1934, in the station area at Gwalior on 21st November 1977. (L.G.Marshall)

3.3 Fit for a Prince! The Maharajah Scindia had his own special bogie saloon for travelling over his lines in the Gwalior area. Numbered 785 by the Central Railway, it was photographed at Gwalior on 9th November 1978. (L.G.Marshall)

3.4 The morning train from Bhind approaches Gwalior on 21st November 1977. The locomotive is no 756, one of the NH/4 class 2-8-2 engines built by the Baldwin Locomotive Works in 1948; the train is decidedly mixed. In 1959 four virtually identical engines, classed NH/5, were supplied by Nippon Sharyo of Japan. (L.G.Marshall)

NONERA

3.5 The Bagnall-built Pacifics of class NM were fine looking engines; all six were built in 1931. Here No 760 pauses to take water, via buckets, from a canal near Nonera while working the morning train from Gwalior to Bhind on the 30th of December 1976. (L.G.Marshall)

3.6 Nonera was the crossing point for steam trains on the Gwalior to Bhind line. On 29th November 1975 NM 4-6-2 no. 763 waits to cross the afternoon train from Gwalior. It was quite normal for the outgoing engine to transfer coal supplies to the incoming locomotive; Indian coal is not very good. (L.G.Marshall)

3.7 While no. 760 was receiving buckets of water from the local canal, the photography party received "tiffins" from the little railcar hitched to the rear of the morning Gwalior to Bhind train on 30th December 1976. The railcar was used for line inspections and it had just been repainted when the picture was taken.(L.G.Marshall)

3.8 There was never a shortage of passengers on the Gwalior narrow gauge trains. NM 4-6-2 no. 760 is seen near Motijheel on a short working from Gwalior to Bamourgaon on the line to Sheopur Kalan on 24th February 1986, with plenty of lineside spectators. It was about this time that diesel railcars were being tried on the Scindia State lines; after all the Maharajah Scindia was the Railway Minister and he needed votes at the next election. (L.G.Marshall)

4. AVONTUUR BRANCH

The line was built in stages by the Cape Government Railways in order to develop the agricultural potential of the area, which was severely restricted by almost non-existent roads. The 70 miles (112km) from Port Elizabeth (known as PE) to Humansdorp was opened in 1903-05 and the remaining 107 miles (172km) of the main line to Avontuur followed in 1906-07. Two agricultural advisers were employed to help farmers regarding the development of virgin land and increasing productivity, railway revenue benefitting as a result.

The 19-mile (30km) branch from Gamtoos to Patensie was built by the South African Railways & Harbour Administration and came into use in 1914. (The Union of the South African colonies in 1910 had brought the change of organisation).

A cement works was built north of PE in 1917 and a 12-mile (19km) long siding was laid from Chelsea for the conveyance of limestone from Patensie. This quarry closed in 1934 and subsequently stone has been loaded at Loerie for a 42-mile (67km) journey, which starts with a long climb at about 1 in 40 for around seven and a half miles (12km).

The first two main line locomotives were 2-6-4Ts from Manning Wardle; these were followed by three 4-6-0s from Bagnall. Six more of this type (NG9) came from Baldwin in 1915 and the firm supplied six similar NG10s in 1916. The 2-6-4Ts were class A and the 4-6-2s class B.

Three NGG11 class 2-6-0 + 0-6-2 Garratts were built by Beyer Peacock in Manchester and delivered in 1919. Three more arrived in 1925. Some larger NGG13s followed from Hanomag of Germany in 1928-29. By 1959, the line had eleven Garratts, including some NGG16s, each capable of hauling 600 tons on the level.

Class NG15 2-8-2s from Henschel and Franco-Belge were transferred from other lines in due course. There were 42 locomotives serviceable by 1962.

The fortunes of the line declined, particularly in the 1960s, with improvements in road transport. There was an upturn in 1985 when cold stores for apples began to be built on farms, instead of only at the harbour at PE. The fruit could be conveyed between the two in insulated containers by rail, devoid of road vibration damage. Further developments took place with improved mchanical handling and wagon design. Much business was recovered from the road hauliers but the citrus fruit traffic was retained on rail.

Passenger services have always been of secondary importance to the conveyance of the products of nature. From the outset, passenger trains have been operated on holidays from PE to various locations for pleasure purposes. With the advent of personal road transport, these declined but one or two coaches were usually attached to freight trains for local passengers. In later years, a coach would be provided only as necessary or upon request. Lavatories were first provided on trains in 1916.

The first entirely passenger service for many decades was run by SAR from PE to Loerie in May 1965. This marked the reinvention of

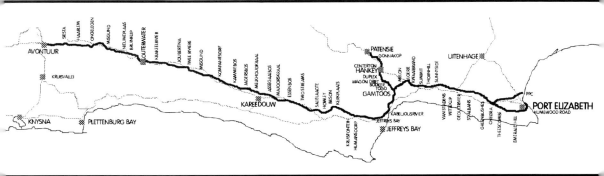

pleasure travel on the line and a train ran every month or so thereafter in season.

Tourist services were administered by the Alfred County Railway management from December 1993 to August 1995. The Apple Express Society was formed on 30th November 1995 and has subsequently operated trains at weekends and on public holidays to Thornhill. A special Steam Safari was worked through to Avontuur in the March of 1996 and 1997. The line continues to be a branch of South African Railways (Spoornet since 1990), which operates all freight traffic.

In the latter part of 1997, there were several trips as far as Thornhill each month, with an occasional one to Loerie. The number of passengers carried in 1996 was 10518 and in 1997 it was 7999, with 68 and 62 trains operated.

Most of the PE-Avontuur route is roughly parallel to the south coast of South Africa but is separated from it by a series of mountain ranges at its western end. The Kouga Mountains are on its northern flank at that end. The combination creates spectacular scenery.

The branch north to Patensie follows the steep-sided Gamtoos Valley, in which is situated the town of Hankey.

Since the first democratic elections in SA in April 1994, most of the railway has been in the province of Eastern Cape. It has attained the status of the longest and thus the most significant two-foot gauge route in the world. The journey is longer than that from London to Exeter.

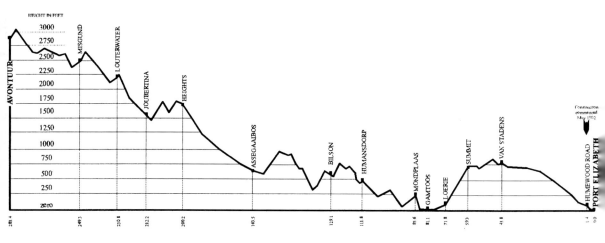

PORT ELIZABETH HARBOUR

4.1 A two-foot gauge Garratt hauls a train of vans across the 3ft 6ins tracks on 29th April 1973. Open and covered exchange sidings are on the right. The acting British governor of the area named the port after his late wife in 1820, when the first settlers arrived. Both gauges ran into a joint passenger terminus behind the camera until the 1930s. (D.J.Mitchell)

4.2 This massive cold store was built in 1984 between the two sheds seen on the left of the previous picture, its unusual interlaced tracks receiving insulated fruit wagons. A flock of fork lift trucks unloads the train expeditiously, penalties being due if the temperature of the apples and pears rises more than 2 degrees Celcius in transit. Pine gum is shipped from PE as well. (V.Mitchell)

4.3 The extent of the railway network could be easily appreciated if one was on the train seen in picture 4.1. It would have descended the 1 in 33 trestle incline on the left and passed round a curve beyond the four sheds in the centre background. That picture was taken from the tower seen between the cranes, which themselves are used for the transhipment of timber between the gauges. (V.Mitchell)

PORT ELIZABETH HUMEWOOD ROAD

4.4 The line on the left of the previous photograph continues to the foreground of this one which was taken at the east end of the very long station site. Centre left is the 3ft 6ins line from the harbour; trains have to reverse in the headshunt on the left having climbed up at 1 in 50. (V.Mitchell)

4.5 The previous four pictures and 4.7 - 4.8 date from March 1997; this and the next are from April 1973, there being little structural change in the interval. From left to right are examples of class NG15, NG13 (in shadow), NGG13 and NGG11. (D.J.Mitchell)

4.6 The right hand line in picture 4.4 continues into the passenger platform featured here. Coupled to a fruit van is class NGG11 no. 54 of 1925. The sidings in the distance are clearer in the next view. Out of view and at harbour level is a short length of 2ft track used for the "Diaz Express" since 1987. This runs at weekends for the entertainment of holidaymakers at Kings Beach. (Diaz was the first European to land here). (D.J.Mitchell)

4.7 A westward view from the station has the running line centre and part of the locomotive depot on the left. This was under the control of the Apple Express Society and was home for their three NG15 2-8-2s and two Garratts, a NGG11 and a NGG16. (V.Mitchell)

4.8 Out of view from the station but close to the main line is the diesel depot, with its spacious maintenance and repair buildings. The radio control centre for the entire railway is also on this site. A fleet of 17 class 91 diesels are based here; these General Motors products can be used on bogies of different gauges. The lengthened chassis on the right was intended for a standard international container and was a prototype for a planned fleet for the conveyance of export charcoal. (V.Mitchell)

PORT ELIZABETH CEMENT WORKS SIDING

4.9 The 12-mile long line was built by the Eastern Province Cement Company in 1927 and was maintained by their own staff using this British-built Wickham trolley. Their first engine was a B class 4-6-0 bought secondhand from the Avontuur line. The second was a new Baldwin 4-6-2, delivered in 1930. (Pretoria Portland Cement)

4.10 The Baldwin's career terminated abruptly when it ran off the end of the turning triangle, due to the regulator not being shut during steam raising on 19th August 1973. The works was taken over by Pretoria Portland Cement. The locomotive arrived in Wales in 1974 and was first steamed in 1998, on the Brecon Mountain Railway. (Pretoria Portland Cement)

4.11 The Baldwin was replaced by a Hunslet diesel locomotive, seen here working empties up the mainly 1 in 45 gradient to Chelsea, a climb of 630ft (192m). In the background are Fraser's Quarries, now long worked out. (Pretoria Portland Cement)

4.12 The original locomotive shed at Chelsea was replaced by this three-road one on the cement works site, although there were usually only two locomotives in it. The Hunslet diesel was replaced in 1983-84 by two diesels built in South Africa by C.H.Funkey & Company. These became redundant in 1986 when SAR took over the operation of the route and were later bought by the FR, arriving in Wales in 1993. When photographed in 1997, the shed housed an oil tanker permanently and two class 91s at night. (V.Mitchell)

4.13 Two more 1997 pictures follow. Trains usually carried 750 tonnes of limestone in 26 wagons, the gross weight being 1058 tonnes After arrival, the wagons are rope-hauled with an electric capstan and individual wagons are emptied in a tippler in the shed. (V.Mitchell)

4.14 After emptying, wagons run into these sidings; a locomotive assembles them into a train and then they pass to the right of the shed. Usually there were 13 trips per week, moving a total of about 339,000 tonnes per annum. (V.Mitchell)

CHELSEA

4.15 Two class 91 diesels, each with 650hp available, negotiate the triangular junction on 18th March 1997 and approach the start of the 12-mile long private siding. The points on the left are to the disused exchange sidings, which were the limit of operation of both the private and the SAR locomotives. (V.Mitchell)

4.16 A view towards PE includes the points (left) over which the wagons on the right of the previous picture are passing. The dirt road on the left passes over two sides of the triangle without warnings or controls. (V.Mitchell)

VAN STADENS

4.17 The bridge over the gorge is claimed to be the tallest in the world to be built for a two-foot gauge line at 254ft (77.4m) high. It is 642ft (195.5m) in length, has 17 spans of three different lengths and required 574tons of steel. This is the "Great Race Train" for the annual Train Race, sponsored for about 15 years by SAR and PPC. About 600 teams of ten runners from around the world compete (nominally with the train!) between Loerie and PE on the first Saturday in September. (Pretoria Portland Cement)

4.18 A visiting group necessitated extra coaches on this up train in October 1968. The NG15 locomotives are nos 18 and 145, both built by Henschel but over 25 years apart. (D.J.Mitchell)

4.19 Class NG15 2-8-2 no. 124 hauled the second passenger train to Avontuur in nine years, the three day journey starting on 20th March 1997. It is passing a down stone train, while disused vans and cattle trucks stand in the sidings. (V.Mitchell)

LOERIE

4.20 Steam was unchallenged on the line when no. 145 was recorded departing for PE in October 1968. Initially running east, it faced a long sinuous climb into the mountainous terrain, mostly at 1 in 40 to Summit. (D.J.Mitchell)

4.21 The tour train seen in picture 4.19 stopped in the platform road for a lunch break and the middle line was occupied by a stone train. This necessitated the up empty fruit container train being diverted along the goods shed line, but a collision with the roof resulted. (V.Mitchell)

4.22 West of the station are the limestone loading hoppers, which are fed by aerial ropeways. These are in the right background and stride across the scenery for almost seven miles to the quarry. This will be exhausted eventually and then the viability of the railway may be in question. (V.Mitchell)

GAMTOOS

4.23 The 1997 tour train would not need the water tanker on its trip on the Patensie branch and so it was shunted to the left. The points in the foreground constitute the main junction on the system, although a triangular arrangement is in place, the other two points were little used. (V.Mitchell)

4.24 Turning round and walking to the middle of the triangle, we see the main lne to Avontuur and the bridge over the River Gamtoos. The first bridge here was of timber construction; the components of the one pictured were made in Scotland in the 1890s and were in use elsewhere until erected here. (V.Mitchell)

PATENSIE BRANCH

4.25 After travelling for 21 minutes up the branch, the tour train came to an abrupt halt when no. 124 ran into a soil washover. There being no roads in the vicinity, the train and its 19 passengers were returned to Gamtoos, 3hrs 16mins later by a diesel. The locomotive was rerailed during the night. (V.Mitchell)

4.26 No. 124 was ready to resume the tour at Patensie at 08.00, as planned, on 21st March 1997. It is here that vast quantities of citrus fruits are loaded; note the vans have had their sides removed and floors widened to accommodate palletised boxes. Roll-down canvas sheets give weather protection. The station was staffed and the well tended gardens included rose bushes and Hanomag-built Garratt no. 81. (V.Mitchell)

4.27 On the return journey on the branch, the tour passed through the sizeable town of Hankey. Within three years of opening, the traffic here was certainly not to be sniffed at. It almost overwhelmed the available rolling stock and included pit props, wheat and maize; large quantities of fruit soon followed. (V.Mitchell)

HUMANSDORP

4.28 The area was acquired by Mr. Human, who started a settlement here in 1849. The grain and fruit loading facilities were recorded in March 1997. (V.Mitchell)

TWO STREAMS

4.29 Set in beautiful Langkloof country, this station is typical of countless others on SAR - a passing loop, a staff cottage and a goods loop, although here only the base of the shed remained. The tour stopped for tea at the site of a proposed charcoal factory, which would hopefully generate rail traffic. (V.Mitchell)

ASSEGAAIBOS

4.30 An early morning eastward vista of the yard and station on 22nd March 1997 includes the tour train, a very rare sight at this once busy location. The locomotive was behind the camera, on the site of the former spacious engine shed, which had been supplied by the tank on the left. Pronunciation is usually "As-ee-guy-bosh"; timber traffic was heavy here. (V.Mitchell)

JOUBERTINA

4.31 In sparkling condition, no. 124 simmers in the sun waiting for tour participants to complete their lunch. Freight traffic here was very patchy and the remainder of the route saw only a few wagonloads of wheat each year. (V.Mitchell)

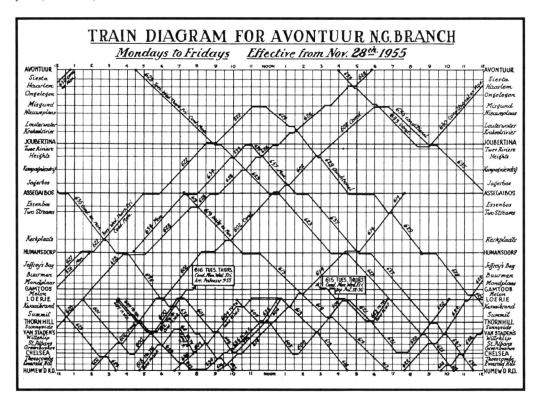

AVONTUUR

4.32 The sun was setting on the third day of the tour, as no. 124 reached the terminus. The extensive trackwork was complete although so little used. Here is the end of the ultimate two-foot gauge journey in the world and a rare opportunity to record stations so seldom accessible by rail. (V.Mitchell)

5. ALFRED COUNTY RAILWAY

The 60-mile long (96km) line south from Durban was completed to 3ft 6ins gauge to the north bank of the river at Port Shepstone in 1901, the bridge over it being completed in 1907. The area inland had been "annexed" by the British colony of Natal and named after Prince Alfred, Queen Victoria's younger son.

Extension at two-foot gauge took place in stages: 24miles (39km) to Paddock in 1911, to Izingolweni 37 miles (59km) in 1915 and to Harding 77 miles (122km) from Port Shepstone in 1917. The hinterland then developed rapidly, traffic including timber, tanning bark and agricultural produce, notably bananas. Later, sugar cane and pulp wood became important.

The first fleet of locomotives comprised seven 4-6-2Ts from Kerr Stuart. Garratt articulated engines were introduced in the 1920s and, in due course, became the main type on the line. Stock arrived from other lines in Africa, when they were either widened or closed.

Passenger traffic withered away and service was withdrawn in 1963, but SAR looked to the tourist market and launched the "Banana Express" in 1981.

Freight traffic declined in the 1980s and SAR closed the line in November 1986.

The Port Shepstone & Alfred County Railway Co. Ltd. was formed and took control of the line on 3rd December 1987, the first privatisation agreement with SAR. Over 10,000 passengers were carried to Izotsha that month. Despite 12 washouts, the entire line reopened for freight on 30th March 1988.

ACR has developed the "Banana Express". It makes one or two journeys on Wednesdays and Sundays (also holidays) to Izotsha. A trip to Paddock is offered on Wednesdays and Saturdays, but Harding was reached only twice in 1997. All these trains are usually of mixed formation.

The general arrangement of the railway has many features in common with the Festiniog Railway. The first section gives sea views; this is followed by a long sinuous climb through superb mountain scenery, culminating in a descent before the terminus. However, the sea is the Indian Ocean, the mountains are the foothills of the Drakensberg, and the province is Natal. Harding is 2900ft (880m) above sea level and 76miles (120km) from Port Shepstone.

Festiniog Railway influence was brought to the line when Mechanical Engineer Girdlestone moved from Boston Lodge to bring experience of gas-producer firing and other developments. The bearings and draughting of some Garratts have been dramatically improved, as have train payload figures under ACR management.

The new company's policy of total steam traction had to be reviewed after three years owing to economics, particularly in relation to the cost and difficulties of maintaining water supplies at the top end of the line, especially in the prolonged droughts experienced.

Two class 91 diesels have been hired from Spoornet since February 1992, but mixed traction has been maintained below Paddock on two or three days a week.

To commemorate three years of successful steam operation and to test run a 37-wagon train, ACR used three Garratts to create a world record for two-foot gauge steam traction by hauling a train weighing 870-tons from Harding to Port Shepstone on 15th March 1991. By that time, the company possessed an amazing 18 NGG16 Garratts and 10 NG15 2-8-2s.

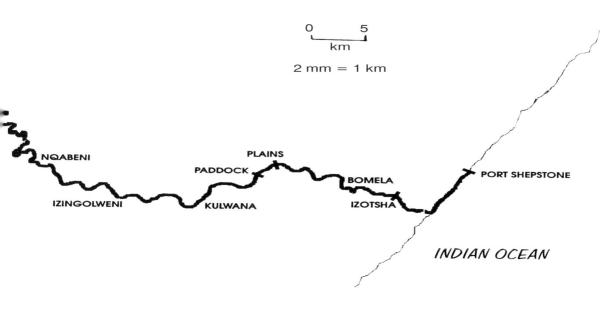

Gradient profile
(Railway Magazine)

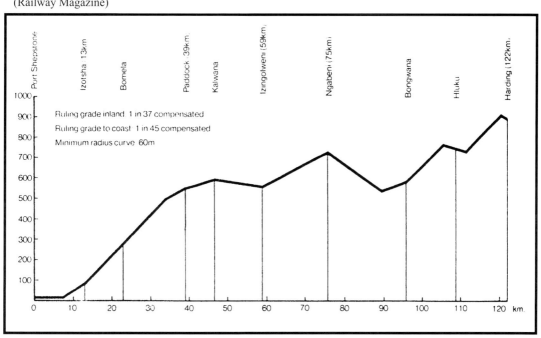

PORT SHEPSTONE

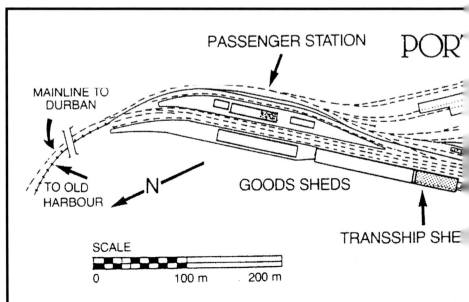

5.1 ← All the photographs of this railway were taken in July 1992, unless otherwise indicated, and they start with a tour from north to south of the freight interchange and locomotive depots. The site is an amazing half mile (0.9km) in length and receives one freight train on weekdays on the line (lower left) from Durban. Featured is the former passenger station and the dual gauge siding to a lime works. The missing lines were replaced in 1994 to enable trains to reach a sand loading bay near the Mzimkulu River. (V.Mitchell)

5.2 A southward view reveals that the engine shed bays are of different widths, this reflecting its dual gauge origin. Electric locomotives were normally stabled on the left during the day, between their largely nocturnal trips along the coast. On the left is the 3ft 6ins gauge yard shunter no. 36-229, while Garratts stand out of service on the right devoid of numberplates. (V.Mitchell)

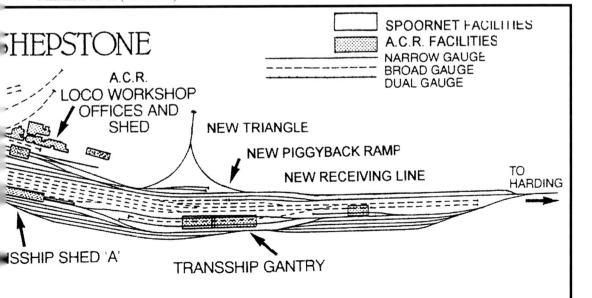

5.3 Looking at the other end of the shed, we see another retired Garratt, along with the narrow gauge yard shunter. This is a 1957 Bagnall, one of three acquired from the Rustenburg Platinum Mines by ACR. The 1992 drought was so severe that drinking water had to be taken inland, three tankers running in an empty timber train. (V.Mitchell)

(Top right) 5.4 The offices (right) almost beat the leaning tower at Pisa for settlement. The well equipped workshops and the stores are centre. No. 10 was eventually reglazed and repainted. (V.Mitchell)

(Lower right) 5.5 The transship sheds are in the background and the restored turning triangle is on the right, as we gaze at another group of withdrawn Garratts. No. 142 is on the left; no. 151 is on the right, with no. 143 behind it. Still more can be seen in picture 5.15. (V.Mitchell)

"NANKA amanzi! Nanka amanzi!" - here is water, here is water - was the cry that rang from hill to hill on Tuesday as the Banana Express pulled into the siding at Bomela. Within minutes people were homing in on the station carrying anything that would hold the precious liquid.

On Tuesday the first train carrying drinking water from Port Shepstone took three 13 000 litre tankers inland, one for Bomela, another for Izingolweni and the third for Nqabeni.

It was part of a scheme instigated by the Rotary Club of Margate to help alleviate the chronic shortage of drinking water in the hinterland of Southern Natal.

While some other areas are being supplied by road tankers, either by the Southern Natal Joint Services Board (SNJSB), Margate Round Table, farmers and other volunteers, there are areas which are very difficult to reach using road transport.

The Alfred County Railway (ACR) passes through some of these remote areas between Port Shepstone and Harding.

Marian Wessels of the Department of Population Development approached the Rotary Club of Margate with the idea of raising funds to pay for the use of the train. ACR was approached and they responded immediately by cutting the cartage rate and offering the first trip free of charge.

They felt it was also an ideal opportunity to extend friendship links with the community through whose land the railway passes.

5.6 A northward vista features the reception sidings and one of two cattle transfer docks. The transverse loading of pulpwood was a successful ACR innovation which increased the payload by 80%. The carriage of 6m long standard containers was also mastered. In the background is the timber transfer gantry - it is in the next three photographs as well. (V.Mitchell)

5.7 A picture from October 1966 shows timber transfer in progress and includes 3ft 6ins gauge stock on the right. The analysis of goods inland (in tonnes) in 12 months in 1982-83 was meal & flour 3822, maize meal 4985, maize 2829, fertiliser 2744, cement 2829, lime 325, creosote 1865 and other 6167. (D.J.Mitchell)

5.8 Maize is discharged between the rails on the left and is raised by screw conveyor into narrow gauge wagons. Maize is the staple diet of the indigenous population and is processed at Ngeli Mill at Harding, where a private siding was laid in 1991. (V.Mitchell)

5.9 These transporter wagons were used by SAR to convey stock to and from the railway works. The innovative ACR developed the principle to convey an entire loaded narrow gauge train direct to the pulp mills at Umkomaas, the service commencing in November 1994. (V.Mitchell)

5.10 This is the view from transship shed "B" to "A". The total transshipment tonnage dropped from 137,203 in 1982-83 and to 72,975 in 1985-86. This is now probably the most extensive such facility in the world. They were always a handicap in narrow gauge operation. (V.Mitchell)

5.11 A final look at this impressive yard includes the permanent way "trolley" and the southernmost electrification mast. Beyond it and out of sight is a level crossing and the new passenger station. The two cattle wagon washing aprons are visible. (V.Mitchell)

5.12 The local authority was involved in creating a new station in 1990, with massive sunshades, close to the popular recreational beach area. On the left is the King Prawn Restaurant and Curio Shop. The footbridge provides a link with the car park and residential area. (V.Mitchell)

IZOTSHA

5.13 Pronounced "I-zot-sha", the station has only some toilets and a loading bank. Stone aggregate was tipped from this into wagons for conveyance to Harding for brickmaking. One passenger train terminated here on Thursday and Sunday mornings throughout 1992, with a few more in peak season. (V.Mitchell)

PLAINS

5.14 Holidaymakers have the opportunity of leaving the Paddock train here and taking a conducted tour of the Oribi Gorge or the Baboon View Trail. A train ran on Wednesdays and Sundays throughout 1997. Note that the driver of no. 141 has a swinging seat, which enables him to sit outside the cab en route in relatively cool air. (V.Mitchell)

PADDOCK

5.15 About one mile (1.5km) before reaching the station, another group of Garratts could be seen stored in the secure compound of the tannery works of D.E.Classen. This siding was well away from the humid and corrosive salt air of the coast. Train control is by paper order and telephone. (V.Mitchell)

5.16 Passengers enjoy a braai (barbecue) while complicated shunting movements take place, as the Garratt will return with a loaded timber train attached to the coaches. On other days of the week, diesels work the full length of the line with the freight. The charming building on the right has been listed as a National Monument. (V.Mitchell)

```
ALFRED COUNTY RAILWAY -PAPER ORDER METHOD OF TRAIN CONTROL
              PROCEEDING AUTHORITY

A. REQUEST. (ONLY TO BE USED FOR INITIAL AUTHORITY FROM STARTING
            POINT)
FROM..................TRAIN NO.............DATE............
AT..................... TIME................

TO:....................
AT:....................

MY TRAIN IS STANDING AT..................READY TO DEPART.
I REQUEST PERMISSION TO DEPART.

B. REPLY AND PROCEEDING AUTHORITY.

FROM:..................         DATE ...........
AT....................          TIME...........

TO DRIVER..................TRAIN NO..........AT...............
THE SECTION ...............TO...............IS CLEAR OF
TRAINS/IS OCCUPIED BY PRECEDING TRAIN NO......WHICH LEFT.........
AT.............
YOU ARE AUTHORISED TO PROCEED AS FOLLOWS:
PROCEED FROM ..................TO..............AND CROSS/PASS
TRAIN NO............AT........................
AFTER HAVING CROSSED TRAIN NO. .........AT................YOU ARE
AUTHORISED TO PROCEED RO ............AND CROSS/PASS TRAIN NO...
........AT................PHONE P.S.
```

HARDING

5.17 The panorama from the rear locomotive cab of an arriving train includes stone from Izotsha, the disused locomotive shed and the blow-down screen (right). The two diesels were uncoupled here and run forward onto the loaded train, as seen in the next picture. (V.Mitchell)

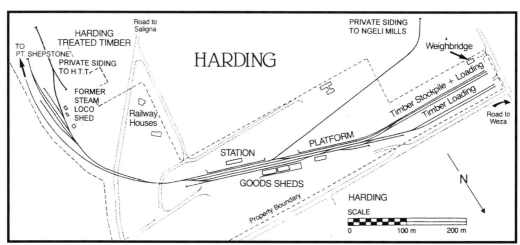

5.18 Dusk was falling as nos. 91006 and 91016 were about to start their overnight return journey to the coast. Your exhausted author returned to Port Shepstone with the train crew by road, in a pick-up in which the night staff had just arrived. Thus the engines ran almost continuously during the working week, moving about 9000 tons of pulpwood monthly. (V.Mitchell)

5.19 The timber train was steam hauled on 17th March 1997 and coaches were attached for a Ffestiniog Travel party. Garratt no. 141 had to bring its own coal and water supply; the last steam working had been a year earlier and for the same organisation. (J.Butler)

5.20 Our final picture of this spectacular railway was taken on the same day and includes Bagnall no. 11, from the same source as the one seen in picture 5.3. The oil tanks are standing in a turning triangle, not shown on the diagram but in use in 1988-91 during the ACR all steam era here. (J.Butler)

6. VALE OF RHEIDOL RAILWAY

The Vale of Rheidol Light Railway was authorised under the Light Railway Act in 1897, its purpose being to carry both minerals and tourists, the former including lead, copper, zinc and some iron ores. Freight traffic commenced in August 1902 and passenger trains on 22nd December following.

The line was taken over by the Cambrian Railways on 4th July 1913, becoming part of the Great Western Railway on 1st January 1923. Nationalisation in 1948 brought it into the Western Region of British Railways, transfer to the London Midland Region following in 1963. It became the last steam worked section of BR and was sold to private enterprise at the end of 1988.

Running inland, the first half of the route is in the broad, fairly level, valley of the Rheidol but the second half is in the narrow, steep-sided and spectacular part of the valley. The eleven and a half mile (18km) long line climbs continuously to terminate near the historic multi-level structure of Devils Bridge.

The first engine fleet comprised a 2-4-0T from Bagnall and two 2-6-2Ts by Davies & Metcalfe, better known as makers of injectors. The GWR built three further 2-6-2Ts for the line at Swindon in 1923; these are all still on the line.

Initially there were four mixed trains, weekdays only. Up to World War I, there were usually six trips in the Summer and three in the Winter, but services were sometimes curtailed during the war. There were no more Winter trains after 1931 but Sunday trains were introduced in the 1930s. Freight traffic ceased in 1937 and the line was closed during World War II.

In the Summers thereafter there were usually one morning and two afternoon journeys. An evening trip was introduced in 1955. This also appeared in the 1972 timetable, when there were five other trains on peak season days. The service in the last year of BR operation gave a maximum of four trains per day at peak times. There has been a more flexible operating pattern subsequently.

For train times -
Tel: 01970 625819
Fax: 01970 623769

Railway Magazine 1947

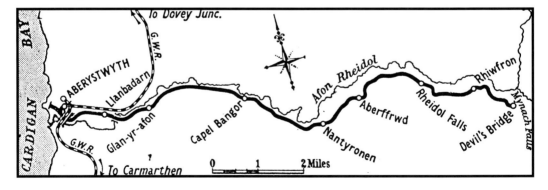

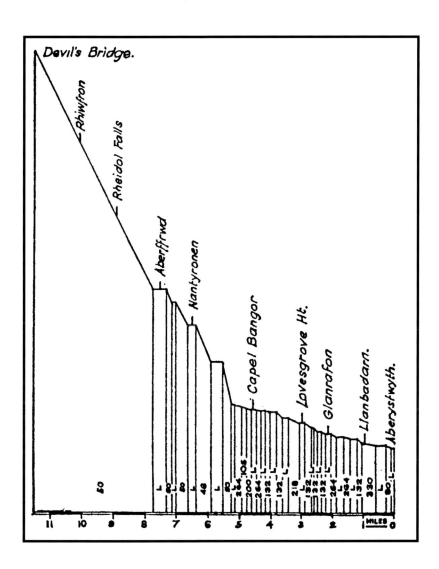

Bradshaw June 1922

Miles	Up.	Week Days only.					Miles	Down.	Week Days only.			
		mrn|mrn|aft		aft					mrn|mrn|aft		aft	
	Aberystwyth ....dep.	7 0|10 0|2 30		6 10	....		Devil's Bridge........dep.	8 25|11 20|4 45		7 30	....
1	Llanbadarn............	7 4|10 4|2 34	Mondays only.	6 14	....	1	Rhiwfron	8 30|11 25|4 50	Mondays only.	7 35	....
2¼	Glanrafon............	7 8|10 8|2 38		6 18	....	2¼	Rheidol Falls	8 40|11 35|5 0		7 45	....
4¼	Capel Bangor.........	7 18|10 18|2 48		6 28	....	4¼	Aberffrwd	8 50|11 45|5 10		7 55	....
6¼	Nantyronen...........	7 32|10 32|3 2		6 42	....	5¼	Nantyronen	8 55|11 50|5 15		8 0	....
7¼	Aberffrwd...........	7 38|10 38|3 8		6 48	....	7¼	Capel Bangor	9 5|12 0|5 25		8 10	....
9¼	Rheidol Falls.........	7 54|10 54|3 24		7 4	....	9¼	Glanrafon	9 15|12 10|5 35		8 20	....
10¼	Rhiwfron............	8 5|11 5|3 35		7 15	....	10¼	Llanbadarn	9 20|12-15|5 40		8 25	....
11¼	Devil's Bridge....arr.	8 10|11 10|3 40		7 20	....	11¼	Aberystwyth 90, 530.arr.	9 25|12 20|5 45		8 30	....

ABERYSTWYTH

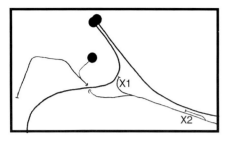 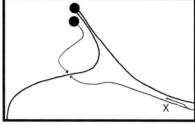 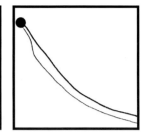

The narrow lines are narrow gauge, the siding on the left being to a riverfront wharf. "X" indicates exchange sidings. The main line on the left is that of the GWR from Carmarthen; on the right is the Cambrian Railway from Dovey Junction. Siding X1 was in use between 1906 and 1913 only.

The 2ft gauge track was extended over a road level crossing to a new station, close to the unified main line one in 1925.

The Carmarthen line closed in 1964, enabling a new narrow gauge alignment to be provided. It came into use on 20th May 1968.

6.1 Nos 7 and 8 stand on the sharp curves outside the 1925 station in July 1954. They were named *Owain Glyndwr* and *Llywelyn*. The trains will depart at 1.45 and 2.30pm, and will meet at the other terminus. The main line station is in the background. (A.G.W.Garraway)

6.2 No. 7 is about to pass under the route of the former Carmarthen line. The site of the first station is obscured by smoke in this 1967 photograph. On the left is the engiine shed, seen more clearly in the next view. (D.J.Mitchell)

6.3 No. 9 *Prince of Wales* was "on shed" at Easter 1968. The siding on the left conveyed traffic to and from Rotfawr Wharf until 1924, the extension being lifted in 1930. (D.J.Mitchell)

6.4 No. 9 *Prince of Wales* was photographed in 1968 outside the former standard gauge locomotive shed, which had superseded the one seen in the previous picture in May. Narrow gauge coaches stand at the former Carmarthen platform in the background. (D.J.Mitchell)

1988-89

Aberystwyth — Devil's Bridge — Vale of Rheidol Narrow Gauge Steam Railway

British Rail's only narrow gauge railway running through the magnificent scenery of the Rheidol Valley.
For further details please contact Aberystwyth Railway Station. Telephone Aberystwyth 612378.

Date	Days of week	FROM ABERYSTWYTH					FROM DEVIL'S BRIDGE			
		Mornings	Afternoons			Mornings	Afternoons		
16 May to 29 May	Mondays to Fridays	1015	1330	1615		1155	1510	1725	
	Saturdays and Sundays	1015	1400			1210	1555		
30 May to 3 June	Monday to Friday	1015	1215	1330	1615	1150	1430	1510	1725
4 June to 10 July	Mondays to Fridays	1015	1330	1615		1155	1510	1725	
	Saturdays and Sundays	1015	1400			1210	1555		
11 July to 2 Sept	Mondays to Fridays	1015	1255	1330	1615	1150	1430	1510	1725
	Saturdays and Sundays	1015	1400			1210	1555		
3 Sept to 2 Oct	Mondays to Fridays	1015	1330	1615		1155	1510	1725	
	Saturdays and Sundays	1015	1400			1210	1555		

JOURNEY TIMES Single 1 hour. Return Trip 3 hours. Break of journey allowed. LENGTH OF RAILWAY 11¾ miles.
All trains on this line finish their day's work at Aberystwyth. Therefore it is not possible to make a round trip with a late departure from Devil's Bridge. Please enquire locally.
All trains are steam hauled EXCEPT SATURDAYS THROUGHOUT when diesel haulage applies. For general notes see front of timetable.
Trains will call by request at Llanbadarn, Glanrafon, Capel Bangor, Nantyronen, Aberffrwd, Rheidol Falls and Rhiwfron. Passengers wishing to alight must inform the Guard and those wishing to join must give a clear hand signal to the Driver.

CAPEL BANGOR

6.5 A westward view in 1967 does not reveal that the river is behind the building. There had been a carriage shed behind the signboard and a loop until the late 1940s. (D.J.Mitchell)

ABERFFRWD

6.6 A loop was added in 1905 but it was seldom used in the 1940s and 50s and was removed. Bound for Devils Bridge in 1967, no. 7 is taking water while its train stands outside the station. The column nearest us was awaiting completion. The loop was relaid in 1990. (D.J.Mitchell)

DEVILS BRIDGE

6.7 Trains arrive on the centre line and the engine then uses the loop on the right. No. 9 has done that on 27th September 1975 and then moved its train into the bay to await another arrival. There had been two more sidings and a goods shed on the left in bygone days. For many years the station was quoted as 680ft above sea level but, when the Welsh name of Pontarfynach was added, the sign stated 639ft. (D.J.Mitchell)

7. FESTINIOG RAILWAY

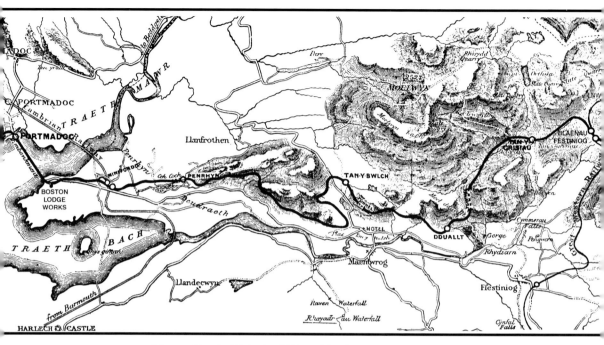

Map used by the FR in the 1890s, with minor cartographical corrections.

Although the town at its northern terminus has two "Fs", the 1832 Act was drafted with only one. Its legal title is used in this volume and was used by the railway until lately.

Recent research has confirmed that the idea for (and much of the money for) the line originated in Dublin, a city much nearer, and far more accessible to the FR at that time, than London. The purpose of the proposed route was to improve on pack-horses and river boats for the transport of slates from the quarries in the mountains to the small sailing ships trading with the ports of Britain and the world. Following completion of an embankment across the Glaslyn Estuary and a harbour at Portmadoc, railway traffic commenced in 1836, loaded wagons descending most of the distance under gravity and the empties being returned by relays of horses. The short length of adverse gradient was eliminated in 1842 with the opening of Moelwyn Tunnel.

Although initially only one quarry used the line for its output, the railway became an immense success. As already stated, steam locomotives were introduced in 1863. This was largely due to the increasing uphill traffic (coal, building materials, general merchandise to the isolated quarrying district) and not, as often stated, to meet the demands of the slate industry, which had peaked in 1856. (The population of Ffestiniog Parish doubled in the 1860s and quarry output subsequently grew greatly). This flow against the gradient, coupled with the return of empty wagons and the haulage of passenger coaches (from 1865), initiated the world's first two-foot gauge steam locomotive development programme. This reached its height with the demonstrations of Robert Fairlie's double engine in the early 1870s, the principle being further developed on the FR. The first bogie coaches in regular use in Britain were put into traffic in 1872; here again the international narrow gauge railway community followed a FR lead.

The FR lost its monopoly in Blaenau Ffestiniog when the London & North Western Railway reached the town in 1879. The Great Western Railway followed in 1882, further siphoning off traffic. Decline followed in the slate industry and the FR suffered similarly. Buses made inroads into takings in the 1920s. Winter passenger trains ceased in 1930 (except for quarrymen) and were withdrawn completely on 15th September 1939, due to the advent of World War II. All traffic over the line ended on 1st August 1946.

The company survived on rental from property and a short part of its main line, despite having had earlier a financially disastrous flirtation with the Welsh Highland Railway. But it had closed this in 1937 "owing to its scenery being incomparable and its lack of antiquity". The historical importance and innovative features of the FR led sympathisers (including your author) to form the Festiniog Railway Society in 1951. The line was reopened from Portmadoc in stages: to Boston Lodge 1955, to Minffordd 1956, to Penrhyn 1957, to Tan-y-Bwlch 1958, to Dduallt 1968, to Llyn Ystradau 1977, to Tanygrisiau 1978 and to Blaenau Ffestiniog in 1982.

From Porthmadog (Portmadoc until 1974) the line runs on an embankment across the estuary of the River Glaslyn, before turning inland and transferring to the valley of the River Dwyryd. The line is on a shelf on its north side and climbs at mostly 1 in 80-86 until penetrating the Moelwyn range in a tunnel. This was blocked before the FR was reopened completely, necessitating the construction of a new tunnel and an accompanying spiral line. The route is now nearly 14 miles (22km) in length and reaches 700ft (212m) at Blaenau Ffestiniog, where there were once over 20 slate quarries connected to the FR.

Four of the original six 0-4-0s still exist, as do four 0-4-4-0 double Fairlie engines, but not all are operational. In the running fleet are two Hunslet 2-4-0s (built as 0-4-0s for the Penrhyn Quarry Railway in 1893), an Alco 2-6-2T and a number of diesels of various sizes. A replica of the FR's 0-4-4T single Fairlie is under construction.

Six or seven trains each day sufficed on most weekdays in the first 20 years of passenger carriage. The figure varied from five to nine subsequently, up to 1929. From three to six appeared in the 1930s, but in the Summer only.

In the first three years of revival six or seven journeys were operated, this dropping to three in 1958 when the mileage doubled. Sunday trains were introduced in 1954. Steady expansion of peak period frequency has taken place, giving an intensive service in high season and only a few weeks per annum devoid of trains. As many as eleven return trips are made on busy days.

For train times -
Tel: 01766 512340
Fax: 01766 514995

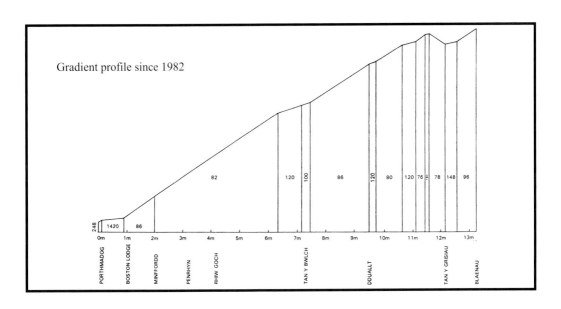

PORTMADOC HARBOUR

7.1 After 1939 the terminus became a dumping ground for a multitude of slate wagons, two coal wagons and two vans. The general manager continued to use one office and collected the rents. (K.Catchpole coll.)

Timetable for August 1893

7.2 The 0-4-0 *Prince* was one of two pioneering locomotives built by George England in London and delivered by sea to Wales in 1863. It is setting out on its mile-long journey in August 1955, the first full month of operation of the FR by its new directors. The original public company still exists. (J.B.Snell)

7.3 Amongst the unusual items of rolling stock acquired with the line was this hearse, complete with internal rollers and external Grecian urns. The chassis of the iron-bodied wagon was also unusual and is shown in picture no. 7.14. (A.G.W.Garraway)

7.4 The buildings in picture 7.1 are in the centre of this 1956 view and those in no. 7.2 are on the right. On the left are some of the wharves and sheds once used for slate traffic, all being served by sidings from the FR. (A.G.W.Garraway)

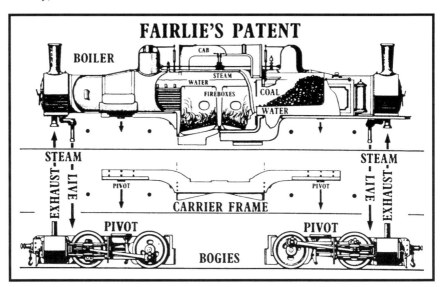

7.5 Now we look right across the previous picture, the former goods shed being in the centre of the view. We are looking from the footplate of double-engine *Taliesin*, the first of Fairlie's design to be put back in traffic, and seen in 1957. The nearest coach was fitted with end windows and ran as an observation car from 1958, another example of FR innovation.
(A.G.W.Garraway)

7.6 The first Beyer-Garratt was built in 1909 and sent to Tasmania. It was repatriated in 1947 by its makers and acquired for the FR for possible adaptation. It is seen upon arrival in the rain in March 1966, along wth diesel 2-4-0 *Moelwyn*, made by Baldwin in 1918. This unique Garratt remained unaltered and was sent to the National Railway Museum in 1976. Work started 20 years later to restore it for use on the WHR.
(A.G.W.Garraway)

7.7 A more useful locomotive for the FR was this 2-6-2T built by Alco in 1917, which arrived in October 1967. It had previously hauled agricultural produce on the French Pithiviers line, one that has recently acquired coaches for tourist traffic. (A.G.W.Garraway)

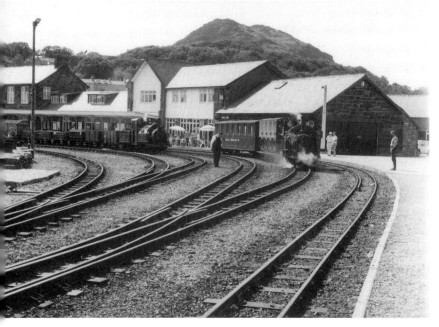

7.8 Immense improvements and extensions to both the trackwork and to the buildings have been made over the years. They were recorded on 5th June 1993 during the "1920s Weekend", when *Prince* was photographed working a demonstration freight train. The 1863 0-4-0 *Palmerston* is shunting coaches. (V.Mitchell)

7.9 The platform eventually received a canopy in 1987. Always keen to evaluate innovative proposals, the FR had a Parry People Mover on trial at the end of 1997. Test vehicle "C" had an engine fuelled by LPG, the energy being stored in a massive flywheel. There was an infinitely variable drive to the wheels. (Parry Associates)

BOSTON LODGE WORKS

7.10 Owing to its early isolation for a generation or more, the FR had to be self-sufficient as far as possible. Its works had two foundries (non-ferrous and ferrous) and workshops of all types. The decaying buildngs are seen in March 1957, with double-engine *Taliesin* in grey primer. (A.M.Davies)

7.11 When photographed in 1960, much of the historic machinery was still belt-driven from overhead shafting. Fairlie *Merddin Emrys* and its top bogie are evident. Modern machines and methods have been introduced steadily. (A.G.W.Garraway)

7.12 A new shed for servicing and storage of coaches was completed in 1992. Right is observation car no. 100, built to a new larger profile in 1965 when the loading gauge dimensions were increased. Left is no. 111 of 1990; visible is its driving compartment used for push-pull diesel operation. This is yet another example of FR innovation on this gauge. (V.Mitchell)

7.13 Top Yard is on the right and the main line is centre as we look at locomotives raising steam outside the former running shed. This was a special event at the Vintage Weekend in 1994. The FR has developed a splendid range of special events each year. (V.Mitchell)

7.14 Always keen to benefit from the latest innovation in railway technology, the FR built a coal wagon in 1880 based on James Cleminson's patent. (It appears in picture 7.3). The centre axle was free to move sideways and was linked to the outer axles which consequuently adopted radial positions when on a curve. The system was a success on gently curved lines, such as the Southwold Railway - see *Branch Line to Southwold* (Middleton Press). The Heritage Group was progressing its restoration when the trucks were photographed in 1995. (V.Mitchell)

7.15 The two Funkey diesels mentioned in caption 4.12 arrived on the FR in 1993. After overhaul and alteration one was sent to the WHR (Caernarfon) and the other was named *Vale of Ffestiniog* on 21st February 1998, the day it was photographed at the main entrance to the Works. Its high level almost centre cab had been removed and a main line class 59 body style was created around its 350hp engine. (P.Johnson)

MINFFORDD

7.16 We look at the area from south to north and start at Quarry Lane crossing in 1957, when volunteers were concreting a gate post. Of particular interest is the unique wagon built for the firm suppling explosives to the quarries. The stores are in the background of photo 7.12. This was a rare example of a privately owned wagon running on the old FR. (A.G.W.Garraway)

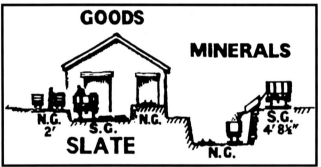

7.17 Following the opening of the standard gauge Cambrian Railways' line along the coast, a well engineered exchange yard was completed in 1872. This 1887 photograph includes the CR signal box and station. The white building was a flour warehouse. All traffic from national stations to Blaenau Ffestiniog was handled here for seven years. (R.H.Bleasdale)

7.18 A view from the bridge carrying the FR over the main line in 1969 includes the slate wharves; these had been supplied by road since 1946. The siding on the right ran to the coal chute; FR stock stands in the centre of the picture. The connection was removed in 1972. (A.G.W.Garraway)

7.19 The FR station buildings were certainly more impressive than those of its main line neighbour. *Prince* waits with vintage stock in June 1994. Note that right hand running is practised. Restoration of the down side shelter was still awaited, 40 years after its remnants were removed. (V.Mitchell)

TAN-Y-BWLCH

7.20 This station has been the midway passing point on the fully operational railway since 1873. The building on the right dates from that time but the island platform was not created until 1968. The signal box was built in 1971 but never used as such. The photograph was taken in 1973. (A.G.W.Garraway)

7.21 The Vintage Weekend of 1994 saw the rare re-enactment of a gravity slate train. Although devoid of slates and unable to start at the top of the line, it made an impressive evening event, the sound of the head brakesman's horn penetrating the rattle of the wagons. (B.D.Mitchell)

NORTH OF TAN-Y-BWLCH

(lower left) 7.22 The views become even more spectacular in this area. The still water of Llyn Mair is seen from the top of Garnedd Tunnel (60yds, 55m long) as *Prince* simmers in low sun in December 1958. The track is in "as abandoned" state. (A.G.W.Garraway)

(right) 7.23 The original Moelwyn Tunnel was impenetrable after January 1957, owing to the creation of a lake associated with a pumped storage scheme for hydro-electricity. The innovation long associated with the FR came to the fore and an imaginative scheme was produced for a shorter tunnel, aproached by a spiral. It starts at Dduallt (seen in 1994, with historic rolling stock) and passes behind the camera position. (V.Mitchell)

(lower right) 7.24 Pictured in 1976, the new tunnel was 287yds (261m) long and was eventually lined with sprayed concrete. Three Cornish tin miners had been engaged for the skilled tasks. Much of the deviation work was undertaken by volunteers and a record breaking 16 year-long legal case was fought for the cost of reinstatement of the railway. (A.G.W.Garraway)

7.25 The dam is on the right, an up train is lower left and Tanygrisiau station is near the white triangle (the car park). This station was the terminus from 1978 to 1982. Some of the massive slate quarries of Blaenau Ffestiniog are in the background. (A.G.W.Garraway)

7.26 A temporary station (left) was created to serve as a terminus from July 1977 until June 1978 and was known as Llyn Ystradau. Now termed Tanygrisiau Reservoir, the water level varies according to electricity demand. The former trackbed is above water level (right). Working a down train is ex-Penrhyn Quarry *Blanche*; her sister *Linda* did not have a tender cab. Neither had tenders prior to their arrival on the FR. (FR Co.)

BLAENAU FFESTINIOG

7.27 The trackwork and footbridge of a new joint station were photographed in February 1982; the platform was completed for the reopening in May. The BR line had been extended from the former LNWR terminus to that of the GWR, using the route of that part of the FR that remained in use from 1946 to 1962. (A.G.W.Garraway)

7.28 The limit of passenger operation of both lines was recorded in July 1997, as 0-4-4-0 *Earl of Merioneth* ran round its train. This locomotive was completed at Boston Lodge Works in 1979; another double engine was produced there in 1992, further confirming the FR's pre-eminence in 2ft gauge engineering. The latter was named *Davd Lloyd George* and was given traditional styling. The ticket office had recently been moved into the Queen's Hotel (left) and a direct foot crossing was awaited, as was completion of a second platform line. (A.Ll.Lambert)

7.29 Having been among the locomotives seen stored in picture no. 5.15, no. 138 was shipped to Britain, along with sister Garratt no. 143, in 1996, for use on the Welsh Highland Railway. No. 138 made its first public appearance on 3rd May 1997 at the FR Gala but was captive in Glan-y-Pwll depot on account of its bulk. The massive slate waste tips serve as a reminder of the material that prompted the development of the two-foot gauge, which ultimately resulted in 61 ton 2-6-2 + 2-6-2s of this type being built by Beyer Peacock in Manchester in 1958. The FR's influence is still to be seen worldwide. (R.Stewart Smith)

Other albums on the Ffestiniog Railway from the same author and publisher: *Branch Lines around Portmadoc 1923-46, Branch Lines around Porthmadog 1954-94, Festiniog in the Fifties, Festiniog in the Sixties* **and** *Porthmadog to Blaenau.*

MP Middleton Press

Easebourne Lane, Midhurst, West Sussex. GU29 9AZ Tel: 01730 813169 Fax: 01730 812601
...WRITE OR PHONE FOR OUR LATEST LIST...

BRANCH LINES
Branch Line to Allhallows
Branch Lines to Alton
Branch Lines around Ascot
Branch Line to Ashburton
Branch Lines around Bodmin
Branch Line to Bude
Branch Lines around Canterbury
Branch Line to Cheddar
Branch Lines to East Grinstead
Branch Lines to Effingham Junction
Branch Line to Fairford
Branch Line to Hawkhurst
Branch Line to Hayling
Branch Lines to Horsham
Branch Line to Ilfracombe
Branch Line to Kingswear
Branch Lines to Launceston & Princetown
Branch Lines to Longmoor
Branch Line to Looe
Branch Line to Lyme Regis
Branch Lines around Midhurst
Branch Line to Minehead
Branch Lines to Newport (IOW)
Branch Line to Padstow
Branch Lines around Plymouth
Branch Lines to Seaton & Sidmouth
Branch Line to Selsey
Branch Lines around Sheerness
Branch Line to Tenterden
Branch Lines to Torrington
Branch Lines to Tunbridge Wells
Branch Line to Upwell
Branch Lines around Wimborne
Branch Lines around Wisbech

NARROW GAUGE BRANCH LINES
Branch Line to Lynton
Branch Lines around Portmadoc 1923-46
Branch Lines around Porthmadog 1954-94
Branch Line to Southwold
Two-Foot Gauge Survivors

SOUTH COAST RAILWAYS
Ashford to Dover
Brighton to Eastbourne
Chichester to Portsmouth
Dover to Ramsgate
Hastings to Ashford
Portsmouth to Southampton
Ryde to Ventnor
Worthing to Chichester

SOUTHERN MAIN LINES
Bromley South to Rochester
Charing Cross to Orpington
Crawley to Littlehampton
Dartford to Sittingbourne
East Croydon to Three Bridges
Epsom to Horsham
Exeter to Barnstaple
Exeter to Tavistock
Faversham to Dover
Haywards Heath to Seaford
London Bridge to East Croydon
Orpington to Tonbridge
Swanley to Ashford
Tavistock to Plymouth
Victoria to East Croydon
Waterloo to Windsor

Waterloo to Woking
Woking to Portsmouth
Woking to Southampton
Yeovil to Exeter

EASTERN MAIN LINES
Fenchurch Street to Barking

COUNTRY RAILWAY ROUTES
Andover to Southampton
Bournemouth to Evercreech Jn.
Burnham to Evercreech Junction
Croydon to East Grinstead
Didcot to Winchester
Fareham to Salisbury
Frome to Bristol
Guildford to Redhill
Porthmadog to Blaenau
Reading to Basingstoke
Reading to Guildford
Redhill to Ashford
Salisbury to Westbury
Strood to Paddock Wood
Taunton to Barnstaple
Wenford Bridge to Fowey
Westbury to Bath
Woking to Alton
Yeovil to Dorchester

GREAT RAILWAY ERAS
Ashford from Steam to Eurostar
Clapham Junction 50 years of change
Festiniog in the Fifties
Festiniog in the Sixties
Isle of Wight Lines 50 years of change
Railways to Victory 1944-46

LONDON SUBURBAN RAILWAYS
Caterham and Tattenham Corner
Charing Cross to Dartford
Clapham Jn. to Beckenham Jn.
Crystal Palace and Catford Loop
East London Line
Finsbury Park to Alexandra Palace
Holborn Viaduct to Lewisham
Kingston and Hounslow Loops
Lewisham to Dartford
Lines around Wimbledon
London Bridge to Addiscombe
North London Line
South London Line
West Croydon to Epsom
West London Line
Willesden Junction to Richmond
Wimbledon to Epsom

STEAM PHOTOGRAPHERS
O.J.Morris's Southern Railways 1919-59

STEAMING THROUGH
Steaming through Cornwall
Steaming through East Sussex
Steaming through the Isle of Wight
Steaming through Kent
Steaming through West Hants
Steaming through West Sussex

TRAMWAY CLASSICS
Aldgate & Stepney Tramways
Barnet & Finchley Tramways
Bath Tramways

Bournemouth & Poole Tramways
Brighton's Tramways
Bristol's Tramways
Camberwell & W.Norwood Tramways
Clapham & Streatham Tramways
Dover's Tramways
East Ham & West Ham Tramways
Edgware and Willesden Tramways
Eltham & Woolwich Tramways
Embankment & Waterloo Tramways
Enfield & Wood Green Tramways
Exeter & Taunton Tramways
Gosport & Horndean Tramways
Greenwich & Dartford Tramways
Hampstead & Highgate Tramways
Hastings Tramways
Holborn & Finsbury Tramways
Ilford & Barking Tramways
Kingston & Wimbledon Tramways
Lewisham & Catford Tramways
Liverpool Tramways 1. Eastern Routes
Liverpool Tramways 2. Southern Routes
Maidstone & Chatham Tramways
North Kent Tramways
Portsmouth's Tramways
Reading Tramways
Seaton & Eastbourne Tramways
Southampton Tramways
Southend-on-sea Tramways
Southwark & Deptford Tramways
Stamford Hill Tramways
Thanet's Tramways
Victoria & Lambeth Tramways
Waltham Cross & Edmonton Tramways
Walthamstow & Leyton Tramways
Wandsworth & Battersea Tramways

TROLLEYBUS CLASSICS
Croydon Trolleybuses
Bournemouth Trolleybuses
Maidstone Trolleybuses
Reading Trolleybuses
Woolwich & Dartford Trolleybuses

WATERWAY ALBUMS
Kent and East Sussex Waterways
London's Lost Route to the Sea
London to Portsmouth Waterway
Surrey Waterways
West Sussex Waterways

MILITARY BOOKS
Battle over Sussex 1940
Blitz over Sussex 1941-42
Bombers over Sussex 1943-45
Bognor at War
Military Defence of West Sussex
Secret Sussex Resistance

OTHER BOOKS
Betwixt Petersfield & Midhurst
Brickmaking in Sussex
Changing Midhurst
Garraway Father & Son
Index to all Stations
South Eastern & Chatham Railways
London Chatham & Dover Railway

SOUTHERN RAILWAY VIDEO
War on the Line